The World's Greatest Predators

LEVEL 9

Teaching Tips

Gold Level 9

This book focuses on developing reading independence, fluency, and comprehension.

Before Reading

- Ask readers what they think the book will be about based on the title. Have them support their answer.

Read the Book

- Encourage readers to read silently on their own.
- As readers encounter unfamiliar words, ask them to look for context clues to see if they can figure out what the words mean. Encourage them to locate boldfaced words in the glossary and ask questions to clarify the meaning of new vocabulary.
- Allow readers time to absorb the text and think about each chapter.
- Ask readers to write down any questions they have about the book's content.

After Reading

- Ask readers to summarize the book.
- Encourage them to point out anything they did not understand and ask questions.
- Ask readers to review the questions on page 23. Have them go back through the book to find answers. Have them write their answers on a separate sheet of paper.

© 2024 Booklife Publishing
This edition is published by arrangement with Booklife Publishing.

North American adaptations © 2024 Jump!
5357 Penn Avenue South
Minneapolis, MN 55419
www.jumplibrary.com

Decodables by Jump! are published by Jump! Library.
All rights reserved. No part of this book may be reproduced in any form without written permission from the publisher.

Library of Congress Cataloging-in-Publication Data is available at www.loc.gov or upon request from the publisher.

ISBN: 979-8-88524-799-3 (hardcover)
ISBN: 979-8-88524-800-6 (paperback)
ISBN: 979-8-88524-801-3 (ebook)

Photo Credits
Images are courtesy of Shutterstock.com. With thanks to Getty Images, Thinkstock Photo and iStockphoto. Cover – Sergey Uryadnikov, Spreadthesign, klyaksun, Tomacco. p4–5 – Martin Mecnarowski, plains-wanderer. p6–7 – Chaithanya Krishnan, Ian Duffield. p8–9 – Sergey Uryadnikov, Sista Vongjintanaruks. p10–11 – Kurit afshen, Algirdas Gelazius. p12–13 – Hayati Kayhan, Anna Dunlop. p14–15 – Love Lego, Pere Grau. p16–17 – GUDKOV ANDREY, Ondrej Prosicky. p18–19 – Peter Kniez, Johan Buchner. p20–21 – tristan tan, Jim Cumming.

Table of Contents

Page 4   Meet the Predators

Page 6   Lion

Page 7   Bald Eagle

Page 8   Great White Shark

Page 9   Alligator Snapping Turtle

Page 10   King Cobra

Page 11   Great White Pelican

Page 12   Red-Bellied Piranha

Page 13   Nile Crocodile

Page 14   Orca

Page 15   Fossa

Page 16   Komodo Dragon

Page 17   Polar Bear

Page 18   Peregrine Falcon

Page 19   Honey Badger

Page 20   Electric Eel

Page 21   Grey Wolf

Page 22   Index

Page 23   Questions

Page 24   Glossary

Meet the Predators

Welcome to the world of **predators**. Predators are animals that hunt other animals for food. The animals they hunt are known as **prey**. Predators all have something in common: to their prey, they are terrifying!

All sorts of animals can be predators. We will look at mammals, reptiles, fish, and birds. Some of them may look cute or cool, but all of them are deadly hunters.

Lion

Lions are big cats that live in a family group called a pride. Female lions often do most of the hunting for the pride. Lions hunt using their sharp teeth and claws. They work together to hunt bigger animals.

Bald Eagle

Bald eagles are a type of bird. They have very good eyesight and can see prey from far away. Bald eagles use their talons to hunt. They eat fish and steal prey that other animals have killed.

Great White Shark

The great white shark is the largest predator on Earth that is a fish. It can grow to be 20 feet long. It has a strong sense of smell. Great white sharks have over 300 teeth to catch prey with.

Alligator Snapping Turtle

Alligator snapping turtles are some of the largest freshwater turtles in the world. They hunt for prey by using something called a lure on their tongues. When prey gets close to have a look, the turtle snaps its mouth shut and eats it!

King Cobra

King cobras lift the front part of their bodies off the ground, spread out their hoods, and hiss to frighten off animals that are scaring them. The king cobra kills prey with **venom**. The king cobra's main prey is other snakes.

Great White Pelican

Pelicans are some of the largest birds on Earth. They are known for the stretchy pouches under their bills, which they use to scoop fish out of the water. Great white pelicans usually hunt for fish in groups.

Red-Bellied Piranha

Red-bellied piranhas have sharp, triangular teeth and an amazing sense of hearing. They can hear prey and smell blood from far away. Red-bellied piranhas are **scavengers**. This means they eat what they can find and don't always kill their own prey.

Nile Crocodile

Adult Nile crocodiles are **apex predators**. This means that they don't have any predators hunting them. Nile crocodiles are known to eat whatever prey they can find. Nile crocodiles even eat prey as large as wildebeest, small hippos, and zebras.

Orca

Orcas are also known as killer whales. They live in family groups called pods. Pods can work together to take down giant prey, such as whales. An orca can make sounds that travel underwater to find prey. This is called **echolocation**.

Fossa

The fossa is only found on the island of Madagascar. It is the largest **carnivore** to come from the island and spends most of its time alone. Like Nile crocodiles, the fossa is an apex predator. Its main prey is lemurs.

Komodo Dragon

The Komodo dragon is the largest lizard in the world. Komodo dragons wait for prey to come close to them before attacking. If prey gets away, Komodo dragons will follow it until it dies and then eat it.

Polar Bear

Polar bears are the largest carnivores to live on land. Their main prey is seals. They hunt by waiting near holes in the ice for a seal to pop up. Polar bears also eat dead animals they find, such as whales.

Peregrine Falcon

Peregrine falcons can be found everywhere. Their main prey is birds. Peregrine falcons hunt by diving at their prey while in the air. They can reach speeds of more than 185 miles per hour while diving, making them the fastest animal in the world!

Honey Badger

Honey badgers are known for breaking into beehives to eat honey and young bees. They have very thick skin. This protects them from the stings and bites. Honey badgers are not hurt when they eat venomous prey.

Electric Eel

Electric eels can make electricity in their bodies —enough to hurt a horse! They use it to **stun** prey while hunting and to scare predators away. Electric eels can't see very well and use electricity to find out where to go.

Grey Wolf

Grey wolves live in family groups called packs. They can travel long distances in one day and reach running speeds of around 40 miles per hour. Wolves in a pack work together to hunt prey that are bigger than themselves.

Index

apex predators 13, 15   scavengers 12
electricity 20   venom 10, 19
groups 6, 11, 14, 21

How to Use an Index

An index helps us find information in a book. Each word has a set of page numbers. These page numbers are where you can find information about that word.

Page numbers

Example: balloons 5, <u>8–10</u>, 19

Important word

This means page 8, page 10, and all the pages in between. Here, it means pages 8, 9, and 10.

Questions

1. Which animals in this book are the largest of their kind?

2. What is the name of the fastest animal in the world?

3. What is a lion's family group called?

4. Can you use the Table of Contents to find out how many teeth great white sharks have?

5. Can you use the Index to find information about an apex predator in this book?

6. Using the Glossary, can you define what a carnivore is?

Glossary

apex predators:
Predators at the top of a food chain that are not hunted by any other animal.

carnivore:
An animal that mainly eats meat.

echolocation:
The location of objects by reflected sound.

predators:
Animals that hunt other animals for food.

prey:
Animals that are hunted by other animals for food.

scavengers:
Animals that will eat dead animals.

stun:
To shock or knock unconscious.

venom:
Poison.